ANCHOR BOOKS

THE WAY WE SEE IT

Edited by

Rachael Radford

First published in Great Britain in 2003 by
ANCHOR BOOKS
Remus House,
Coltsfoot Drive,
Peterborough, PE2 9JX
Telephone (01733) 898102

HB ISBN 1 84418 122 7
SB ISBN 1 84418 123 5

FOREWORD

Anchor Books is a small press, established in 1992, with the aim of promoting readable poetry to as wide an audience as possible.

We hope to establish an outlet for writers of poetry who may have struggled to see their work in print.

The poems presented here have been selected from many entries, and as always editing proved to be a difficult task.

I trust this selection will delight and please the authors and all those who enjoy reading poetry.

Rachael Radford
Editor

CONTENTS

IF I RULED THE WORLD

If I ruled the world happiness would reign
No more cruelty or people in pain

If I ruled the world poverty would not exist
Everyone wealthy, a gold bangle round their wrist

If I ruled the world bombs would not explode
No matter how hard you try, guns would never load

If I ruled the world evil would be no more
Wherever you looked, only kindness would soar

If I ruled the world pollution would vanish
If I saw a deadly fume, this also I would banish

If I ruled the world a smile would be on every face
In every country, in every race

If I ruled the world greed would be extinct
Also, jealousy rethinked

If I ruled the world a wish would come true
You would hear more often, the words 'I love you'

If I ruled the world all this would be true
Paradise for all, made by me and by you

Richard Freeman (10)

POPPIES

As red as the poppies
In Flander's field
Remember those soldiers
Who fought without shields.

They fought, they killed
Until they won
That's why today
We see the sun.

And when all was finished
All people had seen
Were little red poppies
Popping up from the green.

As red as the poppies
In Flander's field
Remember those soldiers
Who fought without shields.

Laura Douglas (10)

THE WORLD

There is a lot that I can say,
About the world, and what happens every day.
People may starve, and even die,
Oh, how it brings a tear to my eye.

Selfish people attack each other,
So loads of people get hurt, why bother?
People are murdered and even shot,
Just because people have lost the plot.

I've had enough of all this war,
It's destroying our planet even more.
But mainly people's hearts get broken,
So I've written a poem as a token.

All those criminals out there,
I don't see why you don't care.
Because the world is delicate and so are the people in it,
So this poem is for you, just please don't bin it!

Melissa Redrup (12)

CATS

Lily is a fast cat,
She likes to chase my cars.
Sweep is a black cat,
She likes to eat Mars Bars.

Sweep and Lily love to play,
Sometimes with each other,
But they occasionally fight,
Then Sweep can be known to bite.

Lily's a really floppy cat,
Whereas Sweep is not,
But I don't care,
Because I think they're really swell.

William Isaac (8)

KIDS ON BIG KIDS

Mum, the best loving, caring person,
She's so nice to my brother and me.
Dad, as bad as grapes with pips in,
So I'm sorry to say he's the baddest man on the planet.
Chris is my step-dad and is as nice as a crisp,
He's the man people would like to see anytime.
Auntie Pat, so good at quizzes, she's great, that's all I can say.
Grandad Dog, he gives me money, he's a gentleman alright.
Grandad Brown, a bit of a bully,
But all the while he's just being a clown.
Nanny Brown is as nice as a star, shining all the time.
Molly, who lets me do anything and everything, she's great.
Carla, my next door neighbour, who helps with my homework.
Peter, as strong as Chris, I think he looks a bit like a wrestler.
Mr Bayliss, so into music and the silliest of all the teachers.
Mrs Widicombe, helpful in every lesson,
Maths, she's just too good.
Miss Collins, the youngest but very nice.
Mrs Penn, the greatest form teacher ever.
Mrs Brinklow, who's just nice, nice, nice and sings like an angel.

Zoe Cox (9)

MY MUM

My mum is like Mars, so high up,
My mum is like fire, so hot,
My mum is like a wire, so long,
My mum is like a teddy, so cuddly,
My mum is like a carrier bag, so strong,
My mum is like a big hag, but not so old,
My mum is like a leech, always stuck to you,
My mum is the best mum in the world.

Sarah Cowgill (11)

IF I RULED THE WORLD

If I ruled the world,
I would be a secret agent,
I would watch bad guys make evil plans,
And then try to stop them as fast as I can.

I would run from tree to tree,
Ducking if I saw a bee,
It might fly into my face,
And then I would lose the race,
And the bad guys would win.

Emma Ritchie (11)

SOMEONE SPECIAL

Someone special is always there,
Whether I am ill or not,
To help me get better and cheer me up,
To tell me not to worry when I broke Mum's new plant pot.

Someone special is always there,
To have a laugh and giggle,
Whether it is watching films or playing silly games,
To teaching me how to dance and make my bum wiggle.

Someone special is always there,
To help me through the bad days,
When I'm stuck and in pain,
They help me through the gloom showing me different ways.

Someone special is always there,
To help me grow and stand by my side,
Watching me grow and progress,
Although they say nothing, I can see their faces are full of pride.

Someone special is always there,
Offering advice, out loud or just a whisper.
You might have guessed already, but if not . . .
My someone special is my big sister.

Isabel Smith (14)

BLOOM OF A WILLOW

The bloom of a willow,
The weeping of the trees,
The raindrops are falling, sparkling in the breeze,
The roses are swaying, the day is ending,
Dusk coming,
Can you picture this rose garden?
Can you picture it now?
The bloom of a willow
The weeping of the trees,
The raindrops are falling, sparkling in the breeze.

Ellen G P Gelderd (10)

(AGAINST) SCHOOL UNIFORM

School uniform is too tight around the neck,
It takes time to get changed,
Mums give up time to iron every day and get tired,
You don't need to wear it every day,
We always wear school uniform and it is annoying,
Please, please do something about school uniform,
No one likes school uniform,
Everyone is against school uniform,
We are against school uniform,
I am so annoyed with school uniform,
If it gets dirty, the teachers tell us off,
And they expect us to get it cleaned in a day.

Ruby Bhambra (11)

WORDS

I've fallen in love,
With words and words,
With only words,
I can describe my life,
The meaning of words,
Come from within my heart,
They come from my head,
The ideas read,
These words of love,
Explains the world,
They pour out of your mouth,
24 hours a day,
The words you cannot keep at bay,
In your mouth they cannot stay,
Words keep repeating in your head,
Even when you relax in bed,
Is that what your mother's fed?
Words coming out like a book being read,
The only thing is
I've fallen for the words,
I've fallen in love with
Words and words,
With those words you judge me,
With these words I judge you.

A Bhambra

MY DADDY IS . . .

A footy nutter,
 brilliant putter,
  a dude on the dance floor.

He likes to have a beer,
 To grin from ear to ear,
  Then sleeps the next day through.

A gadget junkie,
 A bit of a monkey,
  Is this my daddy or you?

Kelcie Gill (10)

IF I RULED THE WORLD

If I ruled the world,
There would be no wars,
Totally, completely peace.

If I ruled the world,
The police could be anywhere,
In a blink of an eye.

If I ruled the world,
The children at school,
Would not wear any uniforms.

If I ruled the world,
The Internet would load
Very quickly.

If I ruled the world,
People would recycle
A lot more.

Alexander Robinson (9)

FRIENDS

They are there for you
Through thick and thin
Always there to listen
Even if you argue, you make up again
You tell them your secrets
Friendships are special.

Susan Stewart (14)

THE ABANDONED PICNIC

In the middle of a wood
A picnic stood,
Just calmly staying,
But why is it waiting?

Under the shade,
The leaves are laid,
All the trees are bare,
Not to watch or stare.

Why the hat upon the tree,
For everyone to see?
The person who disappeared
Has not yet appeared.

Billy Painter (9)

THE HAUNTED SPIRIT

The haunted spirit comes to life,
With his ghostly, glowing phosphorous cloak,
With a skull-like face.
The haunted spirit appears in the street,
With shrieking laughter, a howl in his voice.
The haunted spirit hears the morning bell
And disappears with the night.

Aaron Tomes (9)

THE UNFORTUNATE FROG

There once was a famous frog,
Who did his dance on his log,
One day he tripped
And then he slipped
And fell head first in the bog.

Dorothy Peden (9)

THE SEASONS THAT DIE

The seasons change
All the year round
Without making a single sound
Summer, autumn, spring and winter too,
They all just creep up on you.

The first in the cycle is winter,
The season that is so cold,
It grabs you and keeps you in its hold,
The snow that tumbles to the ground,
Is for you to make a sound.

Spring comes flying to the rescue,
Giving growth to the world when you thought it was dead,
'It is God working wonders,' I said,
The green grass looks modestly through the snow,
I hate to say it, but I told you so.

Summer sun lights up the sky,
To chase away the freezing cold,
So like you, the year can grow old,
Alas! You say it is too hot,
Why do you have to be a fusspot?

Good, it is cooler now that autumn's here,
Now the leaves are golden brown,
Oh, why now do you wear that frown?
Is it too cold again already?
No, just the rain is falling too steady!

The seasons change,
All the year round,
Without making a single sound,
So why do I have to put up with your moaning?
Is there not a quiet way to regard the seasons without loathing?

Stacey Ingram (12)

A VOICE

You're a little voice inside my head
I can't really see you
So you must be dead.

You came to me
In the night
To scare me
With all your might.

Why do you scare me?
Why do you stare?
Why do you come to me?
Did I do something wrong?

You're a little voice inside my head
I can't really see you
So you must be dead.

Lesley Slater (17)

WHAT YEAR 2003 MEANS TO ME

A new beginning to start anew,
To rejoice and worship the whole year through,
For who knows what may be ahead?
Let us find out which path to take
And which promises to keep and which to break.
The new year comes with health and love,
A year to praise the skies above,
But if what I'm saying isn't true,
What may become of you?
Maybe we'll find out in 2004, but then
2003 will be no more!

Marie-Claire Griffiths (12)

THE SNOW QUEEN

Her golden crown
Is as evil as a dark, dark town.

Her long, tuggy hair
Is black as coal in a deep, deep hole.

Her big, evil eyes
Are as blue as the skies.

Her huge, pointed nose
Is as long as a garden hose.

Her juicy lips are red
As a blood-covered bed.

Her bright, white skin
Is plain as a white cane.

Her warm coat is fluffy
As my chinchilla, Buffy.

Her fat fingers are wrinkly
As an animal's that's stinky.

Her sharp, 'knifey' nails
Are as long as dogs' tails.

Her voice is cold as ice
And as small as mice.

Her heart is small as a mouse
In a tiny, little house.

Andrew Mitchell (9)

JEWEL OF THE NIGHT

Little star shining bright,
Guide us through this dark night.
You shimmer like a silver penny
And you are only one of many.
I'll make a wish this very night,
Please help the traveller on his flight.
You will glimmer and shimmer forever and ever,
Don't stop glittering, never, never, never.
I love how you glow,
So sad to see you go.
Now morning is here,
There's nothing to fear.
I'll see you later on
And we'll finish our song.

Belinder Kaur Sandhu (10)

SNOW QUEEN

The soft, icy snow falls gently on the ground,
The softness and the coldness never make a sound.
The reason it is snowing in the month of May,
The wicked Snow Queen makes it snow, every single day.

She has a wicked smile and cold, evil eyes,
One look from her will make you feel like you're about to die.
Her skin is like the ice, cold, sharp and white,
Her voice speaks the darkness of a dark, dark night.

She dresses in the colour of a dark, winter blue,
You're about to freeze when she glances straight at you.
When she talks and hisses, she spits a misty breeze,
Everything about her makes you feel like you will freeze.

Her kingdom is a palace made from clear, crystal ice,
If you ever disobey her, there is a deadly price.
Beneath the icy floors there is a chamber unknown,
From which come the sounds of grumbles and moans.

The soft, icy snow falls gently on the ground,
The coldness and the softness never make a sound.
Why is it snowing in the month of May?
You know, so my advice to you is stay, stay away!

Lisa Carolan (11)

MY BROTHER TARAN

His eyes twinkle like stars,
His favourite toys are cars,
The first three letters of his name spell 'Tar',
He can run very far,
But then he falls over, ha, ha, ha!
He likes shiny things like spoons
And likes to get hold of jam jars.
He gets very hot, such a cheeky little tot.
He loves sweets which he gets as a treat,
But most of all, I love tickling his feet.

Lucinder Kaur Sandhu (7)

IF I RULED THE WORLD

Peace would be the theme if I ruled the world,
I'd make the bad be beaten and hurled.

If I ruled the world, no bad would be unleashed,
And round every corner and behind every door there would be peace.

I'd look on everybody's face and see if they were happy,
The most important thing in life is being a happy chappie.

I'd go around the world and stop fights and wars,
I'd go around opening delightful locked doors.

Ravi Amruth (10)

THE DAY I WENT ON HOLIDAY

The day I went on holiday,
was the most thrilling day of my life.
Sitting in the airport,
waiting for my flight.
But then I asked my mum
if I could have some sweets,
'Course you can my darling,
just don't show them to me.'
So off I ran to the sweet shop,
I didn't even stop,
But then I had a look
at the big, yellow clock.
It was almost ten past ten,
time for me to scram,
So I grabbed my sweets and off I ran,
back to Mum and Dad.
We were just about to board,
when my dad came up and said,
'Do you know where Becky is?'
'Yes, she's up ahead.'
At last we're on our way
to good old, hot Spain,
Hope you have a nice time
in the pouring rain.

Naomi Lewis (10)

REMEMBER, REMEMBER

Remember, remember a time in December
when snow fell over the town
When trees were covered from head to toe
in the whitest possible snow.
Remember, remember a time in December
when snow turned into ice
When the ponds and lakes were as cold as snow
and the sky was as dark as night.

Gemma McGowan (14)

BRACE YOURSELF

I peer shakily into the deep, dark cave, lined with dirty pearls. A foul smelling gas billows out forcefully. I decide the only option I have is to enter. I grasp my only weapon with all my might and I take a deep breath. I start to fit the brace.

Nicola Standley (13)

AT NIGHT WHEN IT IS DARK

At night when it is dark, I hear my baby brother crying.
At night when it is dark, I hear my mum and dad talking outside.
At night when it is dark, I hear the television downstairs.
At night when it is dark, I hear an owl hooting outside.
At night when it is dark, I hear Thomas reading his book.
At night when it is dark, I hear myself breathing.

Georgina Logan Steele (6)

I LOVE MY SISTER

I love my sister
She is very, very kind.
She sometimes has a go at me
And she sometimes does lots of rhymes.
She is very, very pretty
So that's why I love my sister.

Victoria Genever (6)

LISA SIMPSON

Lisa Simpson has a brother called Bart,
And she is very, very smart.
To know all that I do not know,
But her brother is as thick as dough.

She has a baby sister called Maggie
And her clothes are very baggy.
Her dad's called Homer, her mum's called Marge
And Marge's hair is as long as a barge.

One day Lisa was doing her homework
And her dad as usual was being a big berk,
When Bart barged into Lisa's bedroom -
'Lisa you're doing homework! Homework is doom!'

Lisa said that she couldn't care less,
For then at school she'd come best,
'But Lisa, there is so much to do,
Won't you join me sticking Homer's head down the loo?'

'Shut up Bart, you sound evil like Mr Burns!'
'Great, now I can get the money he earns.'
So Bart went away thinking he was so great
And Marge came home from shopping late.

Maggie was with Marge, sucking her dummy
And Homer was trying so hard to be funny.
And so forever the Simpsons will be,
And Lisa and Bart will keep watching Krusty.

Victoria Taylor

IF I RULED THE WORLD

If I ruled the world
It would be a much better place.
If I ruled the world
Wars would not take place.
If I ruled the world
Litter would not be around.
If I ruled the world
Vandalism would not be found.
If I ruled the world
People would be good like all people should.
If I ruled the world
Food would be plentiful.
If I ruled the world
The weather would be beautiful.
If I ruled the world
All my plans would certainly take place.
The world would definitely be *ace!*

Gemma Roberts (11)

KIDS ON . . . BIG KIDS

I am writing about my loving and caring Mum . . .

She loves me and she cares for me,
She understands my problems and looks after me,
She gives me pocket money and pays for everything,
She spoils me at Christmas and on my birthday,
She helps me with my homework and is very supportive,
She does all these things for me and I am writing this poem just for her.
She is like no other person in the world
Because she is my one and only mum,
The most sensitive and loving person,
I am in this world because of her,
She is my mum and I love her!

Hemadri Sachania (12)

MY SISTER LIVVY

I've got a little sister
Whose name is Livvy Loo,
We all really love her
And if you saw her you would too.

She's really, really small
With loads and loads of hair,
It's blonde and curly,
Just like a teddy bear.

She runs around the house
Making lots of noise,
She always makes a mess
When she's playing with her toys.

She bullies me a lot
But I don't really care,
Because she's only two years old
Livvy Livvy Bear.

Chloe Amber Williams (9)

AFRAID

It's OK to be afraid,
Strange things in the dark,
Shadows no one chases,
Trees which turn to faces,
Things no one traces!

It's OK to be afraid,
Strange things you thought you heard,
Or things you thought you saw,
In the dark all alone,
Did you hear it?
Did you see it?
It's just the shadow of the cat next door,
Then you remember the story of the moor.

It's OK to be afraid,
Strange things you'd rather ignore,
But you can't when it hits the door,
Or was it something walking across your floor?
You're not sure!

It's OK to be afraid,
Strange things which are not much fun,
Don't turn round just run, run, ruunnn!

Megan Furber

MY LITTLE DOG, POOCHY

My little dog, Poochy, has a cute little face,
She leaves little puddles all over the place.

She chewed all the furniture in my home,
Till my mam bought her a big, juicy bone.

Poochy sleeps in my bed with me all night,
She chases my brother's hamster and that's not nice.

She likes sitting on other people's dustbin lids,
She nipped Tommy Tucker and he cried like a kid.

She might be naughty, but she really is good,
I love little Poochy and give her lots of love.

Stacey Jayne Aitkin (10)

THE SIMPSONS

Homer gets in his car
And crashes into a tree,
He parks on the wrong side of the road
And has to pay the fee!

Bart gets into trouble
And has to write lines on the board,
'Cause he ate some candy
From his secret hoard!

Lisa is a star
She's every teacher's pet,
She plays a saxophone
And hasn't failed a test yet!

Marge has the biggest hair
It shines electric blue,
It wobbles around all day
Trust me 'cause it's true.

And last of all is Maggie
The youngest Simpson girl,
And though she is not perfect
She's Marge's favourite girl!

Elliot Rippon

RED

Red is for apples, juicy and sweet
Red is for strawberries with sugar so sweet
Red is for peppers, spicy all the time
Red is for onions which make me cry.

Kathryn Biddlecombe (8)

I'D RATHER BE . . .

I'd rather be young than old,
I'd rather be silver than gold,
I'd rather be hairy than bald,
I'd rather be bought than sold,
I'd rather be asked than told,
I'd rather be pushed than rolled,
I'd rather be faint than bold.

I'd rather be alive than dead,
I'd rather be ice cream than bread,
I'd rather be purple than red,
I'd rather be heard than said,
I'd rather be Frank than Fred,
I'd rather be scanned than read,
I'd rather be a table than a bed.

I'd rather be me than you,
I'd rather be Vicky than Sue,
I'd rather be one than two,
I'd rather be old than new,
I'd rather be jolly than blue,
I'd rather be a chocolate than a chew.

I'd rather be . . . can you guess who?

Bethany Becconsall (10)

FIREWORKS

The Catherine wheels are going round and exploding,
making lots of colours fall down.
A Zoom Boom is on the loose,
making an *eeeee* noise as it goes,
then all of a sudden it goes *boom!*

A look book, it's going up and up
and forming a book before I can read the first page.
It closes itself and with a whirl and a twirl
it goes *crack* and explodes.

With a ping pong, a shooting star has gone by
and with a *whizz* and *weeee* it disappears before my very eyes.
But it's not the end of the show so listen,
sounds around you, so sing as you watch them go.

Sheena Cameron

BIG WHITE VAN

Sitting in the front of
a big, white van,
Watching my mum drive,
is more fun than a man.

Looking all around you
being up so high,
It feels like you are nearly
part of the sky.

The van is so huge,
mighty and strong,
We drove past a pig farm,
phew, what a pong.

Our journey is long,
tiring and slow,
Sometimes it's fast,
but we go with the flow.

Megan Cann (7)

A SMALL EVACUEE

We arrived at the everlasting platform station,
As my train pulled up.
Stepping onto the train,
Knowing a new adventure was coming,
For I am a small evacuee.

Pulling away from the everlasting platform station,
Looking back, Mum and Dad a small, waving dot,
Knowing a new adventure is coming,
For I am a small evacuee.

Stopping at a small tucked-in station,
To see big fields and animals I have never seen,
Knowing this was part of the adventure,
For I am a small evacuee.

Looking back on the first day,
Watching the war days pass,
For now I have had the adventure,
For I was a small evacuee.

Hannah Clissett (10)

MY MUM

I love my mum with all my heart,
from my head down to every part.
Sometimes I think she's an angel in the stars,
and other times I think she's from Mars.
There are other times when she's really mad,
but only when we're bad.
She buys us sweets and really nice treats,
she's a really great mum because she even cleaned
                                        my dirty bum.

Stephanie McGarry (10)

PEACE

Peace is the colour of a white dove.
It smells like a field full of sunflowers.
It tastes like a soft marshmallow.
It sounds like the gentle breeze of a summer's day.
It feels like satin silk blowing in the wind.
Peace lives in the clouds waiting for the wind
                        to carry it into someone's heart.

Amie Garforth (11)

THE ENCHANTED WOOD

Dark in the midnight wood,
Owls hooted,
Bats screeched,
I entered the magical mist,
Stars shone brightly,
The wind whistled through my bitter hands,
I watched the silvery ripples dancing,
I knew it was a wishing wood,
I looked at the glistening ripples,
I said to my glowing reflection -
'I wish that the world was no longer polluted,
Please could I ride on a slippery whale's back,
Could people be friendly and caring,
I hope my wishes do come true.'
Then all of a sudden . . .
Silence.

Ruth Colbron (9)

MY BIG BROTHER

My big brother is very kind
I like him the way he is
Although he's horrible sometimes
I'm glad to be his sis!

I wonder how he's doing
When he's working at his school
Did he get detention or did he do well?
But he only tells me when we're at the swimming pool.

I love my brother so much
I don't want him to go
What's that my mum's saying now?
Another brother - oh no!

Natalie Hines (10)

REMEMBRANCE

The poppy sways gently in the breeze,
Lifting petals in the wind,
Its rich, bright, red colours
Will never be dimmed
Because on the eleventh hour of the eleventh day
of the eleventh month
We remember them

The soldiers who fought in both the Great Wars
We will never know what they truly saw
They were courageous and young and very brave
They fought for freedom and their lives they gave
We remember them

The decades go by and the years walk past
The next generation will not be the last
To look back in time and remember the sacrifice
How our young men paid the high price
We remember them.

Olivia Adams (10)

SOUNDS

Lions roar
Larks soar
Bulls charge
I snore
Pigs grunt
Foxes hunt
Puppies bounce
Kittens pounce
Deer leap
We sleep.

Orlagh O'Neill (8)

MY PONY

I have a pony big and tall,
It likes me most of all.
When we go riding down the mall,
I am seen by one and all.
People call as we stall,
Shouting at us as we tread.
But alas, as we go fast,
Our task almost over,
Our pace is faster
For our master,
For the medal to be won.

Terina O'Neill (10)

MY DEAREST MUM

My mum is all I need
The one who will always be there

She has such a pretty face
Surrounded by soft curly hair

Whenever I am feeling blue or down with the flu
She is always there to make me feel brand new

With her enchanting smile that cannot be replaced
I always feel I am touched by an angel

Magical in every possible way
Truly makes her my one and only mum!

Niresha Umaichelvam (9)

FAMILY TIES

I didn't realize the friendship we had,
When you went to Heaven I felt very sad.
When you passed away, my great friend did too,
I felt like my heart had just gone to glue.

When I think of it now, I wish I told you,
'You are the best, John, I really love you.'
Now that you are gone, nothing's the same,
Wallpaper's faded and life's a big game.

You're engraved in my heart with permanent ink,
Nothing or no one can change what I think.
One last thing before you go would be,
Remember John, you're engraved in me!

Bianca Chambers (12)

HUNGER

I looked upon a crowded street
    Watching
As people pass me by.
I want to shout
I'm here, I'm cold, I'm hungry
I don't want to die.

Will no one help me?
I want to cry
I need a coat
I need to eat
I'm cold, so cold inside.

Who will help me?
Who will give me work?
I want to work
So I can eat
That's all I ask for
    From this world.

John Bell (11)

SPRING

When spring comes, lambs are leaping in the grassy fields,
Birds are cheeping beautiful songs,
Buds are appearing on the trees, then exploding in patterns for
                                                    the bees,
Daffodil trumpets blow, telling everybody there's no more snow,
New spring birds are born, playing on the new spring lawn,
Spring comes once more, helping out in the new spring store.

Hannah Leverington (13)

FOOD

Our turkey being passed around
The crackling of the foil, a special sound
The exquisite smell of a fresh Sunday lunch
Going round in the mouth, crunch, crunch, crunch.
Excellent food, all you can eat
Stuffing your face, not conceding defeat
Going and going, how much more can he take?
Plates stuffed full with turkey and cake
Sausages and gravy, carrots and peas
Please, can we have some more please?
Rich Christmas pudding squirted with cream
Been eating for ages, or so it does seem
All this talk of food is making me starve
So I'd better go now before they ask me to carve!

Daniel Hall (12)

THE STARRY NIGHT SKY

The battle of the heavens,
The starry night sky.
The twinkling North Star
Shines down.

The love under them,
The romantic candles are lit,
Of the sky,
The synchronised half of the world.

The light of the unknown
Casts a valley of shadows.
The starry night sky
Is Earth's blanket.

Camila Davidge (14)

THE BREEZE

The trees moved lightly in the breeze
As the wind blew on sycamore keys.
I could feel the wind blowing softly on my face,
It made me feel as if I was in space.

The trees move softly,
The trees move lightly
And the sun shines brightly.

The birds come and go,
The glider comes and goes,
The wind blows my hair
But really I don't care.

Anna Dekowski (10)

THE TRAVELLER

'Is there anybody there?' asked the Traveller,
Knocking on the moonlit door.
And the eagles started screeching in the night sky
And the wind whistled through the gusty trees
While he stood there trembling.

'Is there anybody there?' asked the Traveller,
Knocking on the moonlit door.
And cobwebs hid in dusty corners
And the branches rattled on the windows
While his heart was thumping.

'Is there anybody there?' asked the Traveller,
Knocking on the moonlit door.
And the ghosts were splitting the darkness with their screams
As horses trotted along the misty pebbles
While he stood there shivering in the darkness.

'Is there anybody there?' asked the Traveller,
Knocking on the moonlit door.
And the insects crawled along the floor
And the rats scattered on the ground
As the Traveller turned and ran away and he was never seen again.

Maria-Luisa Gigova (10)

BIG KIDS, SMALL KIDS

A big, wide world for some to care,
Good kids, bad kids everywhere.
We need to let them know we care.
Life can be good,
Life can be bad,
Big kids, small kids everywhere,
We all feel love.
We all feel pain
And underneath we are all the same.
Big kids, small kids everywhere.

Reece Lewis

DAD!

Where did all my hair go?
Did it run away?
Whatever it did, I want it back
And there I want it to stay.
Did someone take it in the dead of night?
Slyly they tiptoed in my room,
Not to give me a fright,
But where did it all go,
The hair I once had got?
Did it escape from my head,
Or did it all just rot?
Did it fall onto my chin,
All to ruin my handsome grin?
I can't stop my head from being bald
And now I feel freezing cold.

S Goodrum (10)

TWIN TOWERS

Planes flying low
Smoke across the sky
Two planes crash
In the Twin Towers up high.
People running, people crying,
People shouting, people dying.
Bodies falling out of the sky,
People watching others die.
Hundreds of firemen searching through the ground
To see if anyone could be found.

As the buildings crashed to the ground
Firemen crushed with a rumbling sound,
Thousands of people lost their lives,
Some had children, some had wives.
Families crying for those they once loved,
But now their souls are in Heaven above.

David Kolodynski (13)

A Thingie

Under the stairs in the dark, dark cupboard,
There's a thingie and he's coming after you!
With a brain like a peanut and claws like a knife,
There isn't much you can do.
He'll creep along the landing
And wave at the monster under the bed,
He'll dwell in the cupboard
And bite off your favourite doll's head.
He'll cling to the ceiling
And dangle over your bed,
So when you climb inside,
He can bite off *your* head!

Emily Allen (12)

ROUND ABOUT THE HOUSE

Round about the house
There are lots of things to see,
Pictures of my mum
And pictures of me.

Round about the house
We watch TV,
One in the kitchen
And one for me.

Round about the house
Children make a mess,
Our mum clears it up
Because she is the best.

Round about the house
There are lots of books,
We read them
While our mum cooks.

Aaron Smith (8)

AUTUMN FAITH

My beautiful friend
Visits each year,
Her presence is wondrous,
You'll know when she's here.

She'll turn the leaves red,
Then make the trees wilt,
Turn the weather chilly
And cries with guilt.

Her brothers and sister
Make fun of her name,
But I think it's exquisite,
Their nastiness is a shame.

Have you guessed who this is,
My beautiful friend?
It's autumn of course,
Beauty itself.

Kirstie Johnson (12)

THE DOODLE-BUG

The doodle-bug, well let's just see,
It's not like the average bumblebee.
Its legs are spindly like little twigs
And it likes to feed on chewed-up figs.
Its body is a big, fat blob
And its favourite drink is human gob.
The spots in its back are not so great,
They're simply there to make you faint.
So if you come across this creature,
Take it to school and show your teacher!

Laura Emily Reed (12)

WHAT'S HAPPENED TO OUR EARTH?

Please read this letter,
It's about the things you could make better.
Motorbike and cars galore,
Traffic jams, pollution, road rage, war,
They kill people, can't you see,
People just like you and me.
Cigarettes, drugs everywhere,
Dangerous rides in the fair,
Help us now, help the Earth,
Think of the day of Jesus' birth.

Aimee Torkington (11)

THE WORLD'S GREATEST PET

She's the greatest pet in the town,
She cheers me up when I'm down.
She sits on the doormat,
She's Foxy, the black and white cat.

She's a little cat of mischief,
She's a cat that likes to sleep in my briefs.
She doesn't like my teacher's pet bat,
She's Foxy, the black and white cat.

T B Manning (10)

MY SISTER

My sister, she's called Vikki,
At times she can be tricky,
But I know when we get along,
We enjoy to play and sing a song.

We both argue quite a lot,
We shout about what's right and what's not,
But I love her very much
And no one can spoil that loving touch.

Beth Sinclair (9)

SCREAM

Here he comes with his blood-dripping knife
Ready to annihilate someone's life.
He wears a cloak of black,
He doesn't hunt in a pack.
His face is that of a ghoul,
He picks off unsuspecting fools.
Blood that stains the carpet floor
And he'll do it more.
No one can stop him,
He's *Scream!*

Kane Watson (10)

THE THREE LITTLE PIGS

The three little pigs were sent trotting off by their mother.
The first little pig made a house out of straw.
I wonder what happened to the other?
The second pig met a man with a twig or two
And built his house out of that,
Now the third pig made his house out of brick,
That made the others look like *tat!*

One day three months later, Mr Wolf came by
And discovered the pigs were there.
Next day, he came to the first pig's house
And to get in he would shred and tear.
The wolf went to the second house and
Thought he'd scare him with a clockwork mouse.
The wolf set the mouse off, heard the pig squeal
And shouted, *'Get out of your house!'*

The third pig had a brilliant plan . . .
When the wolf came, pig three let him in and then . . . *bang!*
Pig three hit him on the head with a frying pan.
(The wolf is unconscious in Animal Hospital).

Lewis Crossley (10)

WINTER

It's cold winter all around,
Snow and ice are on the ground,
Children making icy snowballs,
Laughter and excited calls.
Inside houses, people all warm,
Outside, people in a cold storm,
Icicles hanging like lions' claws,
Icy frost on people's doors.
People all snug and warm,
While outside there's a winter storm.

Laura Casson (11)

CAULDRON SONG

Toads, rats, leeks, oh how much the cauldron reeks!
Fish tail and rotten egg and a bit of Duncan's leg.
Smelly socks and a dead fox,
Rat tail and radishes, as well as cabbages.

Scott Booth (10)

THE THREE LITTLE PIGS!

Now the three little pigs, they were singing a song,
Then their mother said they had to be gone.
Now the three little pigs, they were ever so good,
They started walking off into the neighbourhood.
Then they met a man with straw and sticks,
Oh yeah, I forgot the man with the big, strong bricks.
Then a wolf came along and huffed and huffed
Then he blew down the straw with a little bit of puff.
Then the little pig's house was unable to fix,
So he ran to his brother to see how he did with the sticks,
Then a wolf came along and he huffed and huffed,
Then he blew down the sticks with a little bit of puff.
Then they both realised it was no good with the sticks,
So they ran to their brother to see how he did with the bricks.
Then the wolf came along and he huffed and huffed,
This time no good with a little bit of puff.
To find a way inside, he took a dive,
Jumped down the chimney and was boiled alive!

Georgann Law (11)

THE THREE LITTLE PIGS

The mother pig said to her piglets,
'Come on now, it's time to go.'
The first pig built his house out of straw
With a little, wobbly door.
The second pig made his house with sticks
And his brother made his out of bricks.
Then the wolf came along singing a little song,
'Little pig, little pig, please let me in,'
So the little pig replied,
'Not by the hair on my chinny chin chin.'
So the wolf huffed and puffed and blew the house in
And gobbled up the pig with a great big grin.

Pig number two made his out of sticks,
Then the wolf came along and gave it some kicks.
Oh how the little pig did frown
An the house just came tumbling down.
The little pig wanted to run away,
But he was too late and he got ate.
The third pig's house came and the wolf went insane
By trying to blow down some bricks.

On the roof the wolf did jump,
Down the chimney he fell with a great big bump,
Into the pot that bubbled so hot.
The little pig was making a cuppa
When the wolf fell into the pot,
So he ate it for supper.

Paige Naylor (11)

THE HURRICANE

It's getting late; it's rather dark,
The sky's an eerie grey,
I've just been playing in the park,
A storm is on its way.

The rain is getting heavier
And brighter is the lightning,
I wouldn't normally feel like this,
I think it's rather frightening.

The wind is getting faster,
Picking up its pace,
The leaves are dancing frantically,
One hits me in the face!

I've picked my feet up off the ground
And started heading home,
Now I'm thinking to myself,
I don't like to be alone.

Everyone is safe indoors,
Cosy by the fire.
If I tell them my adventure,
I may be called a liar.

The thunder is much louder now,
I wish I were at home.
My clothes are torn, I lost my hat,
God, Mum is going to moan.

I've reached my destination,
I'm hurled through the door.
'Where have you been, young man?'
I collapse upon the floor.

'A hurricane, a hurricane, a hurricane!' I said.
'Now don't go telling porky-pies,
Go straight up to bed!'

Charlie Moore (10)

THE SEA

The sea flows back and forth
Across and onto the coast it gushes,
The wind sounds so chilling, like a howling wolf
As the waves skip towards me.

Waves crash upon the rocks,
Swaying to and fro,
If I could capture the salty smell in a special box,
I would take it home with me.

The sea is a home to some wonderful creatures,
Dolphins, fish, sharks, whales and urchins
And plants with strange-looking features.
It makes me feel happy.

Emma Fretwell (10)

THE HURRICANE

The hurricane came howling, howling down the street,
Picking up everything that it could see.
It lifted all the houses and then all the cars,
Spun them round and round and sent them to Mars.

The hurricane was drifting, drifting from left to right,
Heading down towards the coast to give people a fright.
It pushed and pulled their clothes and put sand up their nose.
It blew the football across the pitch and into the other team's goal.

The hurricane was wailing, wailing like a ghost,
The children stayed in the warm, eating soup and toast.
The power lines smashed, falling to the ground,
Leaving the town in darkness, giving children frowns.

Jake Morgan (11)

SNOWSTORM

The snowstorm rages all night long,
Singing such an eerie song,
Coating the trees with cotton wool buds,
Killing off the vegetable patch, including the spuds.

This shows that winter has arrived,
Bringing with it the will to survive.
Birds have gone to find a place in the sun,
But they'll be back when winter has done.

Rapping on the window while we're in bed,
Just what the weatherman previously said.
The snowstorm rages all night long,
But mysteriously, in the morning the snow has all gone.

William Corderoy (10)

THE SEA

The sea was
Crashing on the shore,
Kicking up the stones,
Bullying the rocks,
During the storm.

The sea sounded like
The crashing of a car,
The banging of a drum,
The shaking of a shaker
During the storm.

The sea looked like
It was jumping up and down,
Dancing in the air,
Playing with an invisible ball
During the storm.

The sea
Started by jogging,
Settled to walking,
Until it rested
After the storm.

Tasha Berbank (11)

THE HURRICANE

There it was, a horrid sight,
A hurricane wanting to fight.
Dark and grey, spinning fast,
Its gloves were on, ready to blast.

Twisting, turning, swirling, curling,
The hurricane began its attack,
Knocking down trees and blowing off roofs,
The rapid spinner carried on.

A dinosaur, crushing all in its path,
Revolving rapidly, manoeuvring
Everything in its way.
Eventually it stopped
And laid down and died.
The horrible hurricane was over!

Kristian Smith (10)

WHO AM I?

I come when it's cold and wet outside,
So stay in the warm by the fireside.
I arrive in the day or at night,
I can howl like a wolf and give you a fright.
    Who am I?
I envelop your car and smother the ground,
The things that I cover will not be found.
I twirl and swirl and whistle like you,
But if you come out then I'll turn your lips blue.
    Who am I?
Have you guessed who I am
From the things you've been told?
I'm blustery, white and very cold.
The dead of winter is when you'll meet me
And then you'll discover my identity.
    Who am I?

Laura Hodgkins (11)

THE FOG

The ghostly fog silently creeps through the deserted streets.
Stealthily it envelops everything in its way,
A thick blanket weaving in and out of the houses,
Like a slithering snake searching for its prey.

The shapeless, noiseless fog hovers over the voiceless water,
Swiftly covering every victim in its path,
Invading the land with calm control,
Then suddenly pouncing, declaring its wrath.

Fading, faintly, weakly relenting
As its anger slowly disappears.
The sun reappearing to destroy its enemy
As its victims are free from their fears.

Hayley Crouch (11)

THE SNOWSTORM

Gracefully and gently the snow cloud wept,
The tears on his cheek were icy and wet.
Slowly and softly the snowstorm began,
By the tears from his cheek and a wave of his hand.

Silent but restless, the snowflakes drift down,
Lonely but happy, they float to the ground
Like a shower of shooting stars covering the Earth
Or a million new babies, witnessing their birth.

Elizabeth Worth (10)

OBSERVING AUTUMN

Red, yellow, orange and green,
Lots of colours to be seen.
I go *crunch, crunch* in the leaves
As I feel the autumn breeze.

When the conkers fall from the tree,
Children start to shout with glee.
With their cases so spiky and dark,
Playing conkers is such a lark.

When autumn comes, back go the clocks,
No more wearing pretty frocks.
Dark in the morning, dark at night,
On Hallowe'en we get a fright.

We go to see the fireworks,
In the darkness anything lurks.
On the bonfire the flames leap high,
Then the fireworks shoot to the sky.

Kirsty Swarbrick (10)

MY LOVELY NANNY

My nanny is always happy,
Her smile lights up the room,
She's always lucky when she sees the new moon.
She is never sad or upset,
But likes to wear her hair net,
With curlers and clips in her hair,
She is always very right and fair.

Her cakes are so divine,
She should have autographs to sign.
Everyone knows her glowing face,
Walking down the high street at her own pace.
Wallington is where she shops,
Browsing skirts, trousers, stockings and tops.
To win the lottery would be her dream,
In sports cars she would ride to visit the Queen.

I love you Nanny, with all my heart,
You're so funny, wise and smart.
Thank you Nanny, for all you do,
But today's the day when we serve you.

Rachel Beresford-Ward (14)

WHEN I GROW UP

When I grow up
I want to be
As light as
A flea.

When I grow up
I want to be
By the
Sea.

When I grow up
I want to be
Able to own
My own key.

When I grow up
I want to be
A buzzing
Bee.

When I grow up
I want to be
Able to make
A cup of tea.

When I grow up
I want to be
Married to
A Leo.

When I grow up
I want to be
Well, just
Me!

Vicki Ford (14)

MY MUM AND DAD

My mum and dad are the best,
Like two birds in a nest.

When I saw I couldn't believe
How good it could be.

They're two pieces of heather,
Sat together.

Ryan McAnerney (10)

KIDS ON BIG KIDS

I have this favourite teacher,
She always makes me smile.
When she's gone on holiday,
She won't be gone for a while.
She teaches me some new work
And how to remember it too,
But now she's gone away
On her fantastic holiday,
But then she said to me,
'I'll come back to stay.'
My teacher's name is Miss Brown,
She's really, really great.
She's my teacher today
And my friend tomorrow.

Sheun Oshinbolu (10)

IF I RULED THE WORLD

If I ruled the world, I would:
Have one year off if I had a bad cough.
I'd get one million pounds for every sum I got right,
I would stay up late, even on a school night.
I would have Indian food every day,
I would have an eight-bedroomed house every May.
If I ruled the world, I'd have everything!

Emma Pilling (10)

HAPPINESS IS . . .

Happiness is about love and cherishing
and staying together forever,
and drops of sunlight filling the clear blue sky.
Happiness is when you gaze and fall
head over heels in love
and when you dream about the
happiness of the future when you are little.
Happiness is when you get married
and will be together forever
and have little plans of hope for weddings.
Happiness is when you look forward to having a baby
and when you see it gaze into your eyes.
Happiness is when your baby says its first word, Mummy.

Bryony Greenway (9)

IF I RULED THE WORLD

Environment.
We use trees as if they're going out of fashion,
And we don't know how little there is left.
Oil,
Coal,
Unrenewable resources
Will one day be gone
And what will be there for the future generations?

Nothing,
The world will be empty
Except for people,
Walking on dust.

Have you ever wanted to save the world?
You choose.

Sarah Hamill

SPACE

Outside Earth's atmosphere
Is a place most people really fear.
Whether to believe or not
That wee green men make up plots.

Millions and millions of miles of nothing,
Nothing at all,
All apart from the galaxies and Milky Way, stars,
The sun and moon and planets.
Planets, there are nine,
Earth, Mars, Neptune, Uranus,
Jupiter, Saturn, Venus, Mercury and Pluto.

Pluto is the coldest one as it is furthest from the sun.
Mars is really quite scary, but not at all hairy.
And to tell the truth, *Earth* is number one!

Ashleigh Hamilton (13)

ANIMALS

The little dog howls in the middle of the night,
Giving the night birds a bit of a fright,
In the field gallops a beautiful horse,
In the aviary, pretty birds fly of course.
The fluffy sheep guard the prancing, little lambs
And keep a good lookout for big, handsome rams.
A sweet little mouse hides in a dark hole,
Under the earth is a funny little mole.
The speedy cheetah runs away,
The small kittens just love to play,
A giraffe sighs and chews on a twig,
A ginger rabbit puts down his nose to dig.
The elephants roll in a bath of mud,
The gentle cow chews on the cud,
A small, dainty bird sings in a tree,
My loving cat is here for me.
The silver fish swim in the sea,
Then there's a bee, the size of a pea.
I love the big, white polar bear
That gives the fat, lazy seals a scare.
A snake slowly slides over the sand,
A camel can go over a lot of land,
The ducks quack and eat their bread,
A swan holds up her graceful head.
Tigers have a place in my heart,
The obedient donkey pulls a cart,
A blue dragonfly hovers over the water,
The quiet doe protects her daughter.
All these creatures are like a big shiny gem,
Who would ever want to hurt them?

Rachel Lisk (12)

CAT

Her name is Sweep,
She likes to peep
At you through the window,
At night when you are asleep.

You open the door,
She skids on the floor,
Trying to get to her favourite place,
Underneath the fireplace.

At half-past seven,
She's in heaven
Running around the room,
Listening to her favourite tune.

She's my favourite cat,
I can tell you that.
She loves her box,
But hates the fox!

Alice Isaac (12)

DREAMS

Small children's little faces
Look upon so many places,
To the sky and out to sea,
Travel there with you and me

For in their dreams they travel far,
Trying to catch a falling star
And as they lie asleep in bed,
Marvellous thoughts surround their head.

Far distant forests and up in space
I wonder what is in that place?
For they can reach it in a dream,
As it is real, or so it seems!

Rebecca Farrugia (12)

SECONDS OF A CLOCK

How would it feel to be time,
The answer to everything?
I would be the reason for being late,
The reason for worry.
Oh, what a life it would be.

How would it feel to be time?
To keep moving my arms,
No stopping for a second,
Never allowed to stop.
Oh, what a life it would be.

How would it feel to be time?
When I stop forever,
I am not given a second look,
In the bin I go.
Oh, what a life it would be.

How would it feel to be wished time,
The reason for happy times,
Keeping everything ticking,
Bringing smiles on faces.
Oh, what a life it could be.

Indresh Umaichelvam (12)

STAND AND STARE

As the day rises up
I step outside with the wind in my hair
All I can do is stand and stare

I hear voices, as I push open the gate
I see children buying sweets to share
All I can do is stand and stare

The chimes were singing
In the light air
All I can do is stand and stare

I see poor people sitting on the path
As they beg for money to spare
All I can do is stand and stare

I'm home now
I'm back there
All I can do is stand and stare

Bianca Bewley (13)

IF I RULED THE WORLD

My heart and what it says -

There'd be no war
Leaving streets like an apple core
I'd make sure they'd never come back
'Cause I'd show them the way to his or her door.

By the time I count to four
I'd also make it part of the law
That guns galore
Would not be legal any more.

Oh no!

Zachariah James Gachette (12)

DISCUSSION

Discussion everywhere
Fallen leaves of trees grown bare
Peeling bark of the tree stumps
Blossom fallen in great lumps
Shattering into the air
I barely feel it's even there
Decaying nature under foot
Trees starting to carry fruit
The veined leaves drop
Right from the top of the tree
Which I can clearly see
The mixed aromas of the wood
Birds twittering as they should
Trees with tales to tell
Like what's at the bottom of the wishing well
I feel the cold, crisp air
Underneath Mother Nature's watchful stare

Holly Jasmine Rogers (10)

MY SPECIAL FRIEND

A friend who is like my family,
A friend who is in my heart.
A friend who has always been with me
We will never break apart.
My friend and I together,
My friend who knows me so,
My friend who will be my friend forever
My friend will never go.
For nine years together
Still nine or more to come.
I know we will both think
These years have been such fun.
My special friend, the friend to me,
Friends till the day we die
We'll never fight
We'll never scream.
We'll never fall out or cry.

Sharna Holman (12)

GRANDA

I lie in my bed and I think about you,
What we have is so very true.
I know that someday I will see you again.
Now we're apart, I will always remember you
I miss you so much and I know that you do too.
I will always remember you.
When I feel you in my heart,
I know I have to live without you in my life,
But I will always remember you.
So many days pass through the year,
Sometimes I would cry myself to sleep.
I never realised how much I loved you.
If you were to come back, I would
Hug and kiss you.
I will always remember you.

Abby Foster (11)

THE LAKE

The lake played a lullaby clear and sweet,
Whilst the rushes played a deep, brass sound.
Beside the rippling water, a mournful hoot was heard
The great northern diver just waiting to be found.

Under the water:

The rainbow headed drake, dabbled furiously
To reach just a mouthful of the green, speckled weed.
The small swerving fish darted through the fronds,
Swimming from the duck, desperate for a feed.

Down in the deep, a great pike was seen,
Silently skimming the silky mud.

Joanne Frances Riggall (8)

Swimming Party

There is a swimming party but I don't know when
or what time?
It is on Wednesday, the day before Sunday
At 1.62 in the afternoon.

Please don't come, you'll enjoy yourself
We'll let you in but don't stay in.

We'll pay for you, but you pay at the door
You will need a swimsuit but don't take it out
of the house. Please!

Karen Dey (11)